FIND YOUR STYLE, FIND YO

Author: Rosie Huckle
Copyright: ©Rosie Huckle, 2018

Introduction

As we go through life, things change. We may get married; have kids, change careers or start a business. Our body can change too – especially after having kids or post menopause. So it makes sense that as our life and body changes, the way we dress and our style will too. What we wore in our 20's may no longer flatter in the same way or feel appropriate as a busy mum; or as we move into our 40's, 50's and beyond.

For many women, this can leave them feeling lost and confused about their style and worrying about what to wear can really knock their confidence. When our confidence is low, it can impact so much in our lives; how we socialise, how we show up in our relationships, and even how we progress our careers.

I passionately believe that when we know we look great, we feel great! Our confidence levels soar and we feel more able to step outside our comfort zone and live our lives to a fuller extent.

Getting to grips with your style and loving how you look can really increase your confidence and have a ripple effect through other areas of your life.

What would you do if you had more confidence?

Does this sound like you?

Many of the women that I work with often just feel lost and overwhelmed when it comes to their style. They know that they want and need to make a change, but they just don't know where to start. They will go shopping but often feel that the stores they go to no longer have anything for them. The result being that they either come away empty handed and feeling even more frustrated, or they buy something "that will do" but doesn't make them feel good; and often is a repeat of something that they already have in their wardrobes. It may be an item that they may never wear and certainly does nothing to increase their confidence levels; which just makes them feel worse.

This shows up in one of two ways. Either they end up with wardrobe(s) full of clothes but still feel that they have nothing to wear as nothing feels "like them" or they have a wardrobe that is almost empty as worried about making yet another mistake, they just don't buy.

No matter your age, shape or size, you can look fabulous - and feel fabulous about how you look – every single day.

Shopping can be easy and getting dressed can be fun!
Imagine going shopping and easily being able to filter out the clothes that don't suit you – before you get into the changing room. No longer feeling completely overwhelmed when you walk into a Department Store not knowing where to start and no more heartache of trying on one outfit after the other that just does not fit or suit you.

Imagine being able to build up a compact collection of clothes that easily go together making picking out what to wear, super easy and enabling you to get more outfits from less items.

And last but most importantly, the clothes that are in your wardrobes are those that you love to wear, make you feel confident and that you look amazing in. Getting dressed becomes easy.

The days of trying on several outfits, taking them off and throwing them on the bed before leaving the house feeling disheartened and frustrated will be over.

You do have "a style", I promise you!
Many of my clients feel that they have lost their style and they just simply do not have one any longer. This is just not true! You do have a style; you are just not clear about what it is yet but this is the most important part of creating a wardrobe of clothes that you love. When we are not clear on what our style is, we buy clothes without too much thought and end up with a really confused wardrobe; I see this a lot when I carry out wardrobe edits with my clients.

Your style is simply the kinds of clothes that you love to wear, that make you feel, well, like you! For some, comfort is a word they would use a lot and for them clothes must be in soft fabrics and be comfortable to wear. They will often go for a flat rather than a heel, a boot rather than a shoe, minimal make-up and a hairstyle that requires little maintenance. Whilst, someone else will happily spend an hour or two getting ready for their day; curling their hair and perfecting their make-up and nails. They may love details on their outfits opting for glitter, sequins, frills or bows and would always opt for a heel if possible. However, if you swapped these ladies outfits and put them in each other's clothes, even if the colours and styles were flattering on them, they would just simply feel uncomfortable and self-conscious. Sound familiar?

Getting clear on what your style is, is a process that can take a little time but is worth it both in terms of finance and confidence. To start this process, either create a Pinterest board or a scrapbook and fill it with image of outfits and celebrities whose style you admire. Don't go thinking about what will suit you or what you think can wear, this is just about you noting what it is that you like. Once you have done this, sit back and look for similarities in the images. What are the things that these all have in common?

So, when I trained as a Stylist, having completed my training, I took myself on a shopping trip and I bought clothes in colours and styles that suited me and pleased with my new wardrobe I started to wear them and put together outfits. And I got compliments - all the time; it was brilliant! However, to my surprise, I still found that I had items that I rarely or never wore and there were other items that I would happily wear everyday it was possible. This got me thinking into why with my new skills, was I still spending money on clothes that didn't feel right when I wore them?

So, I went through the same process above. I created a Pinterest board and every time I saw an item or an outfit that I liked, I pinned it to my board. A few weeks later, I sat with a cup of tea and looked at what I had pinned. The results of what I found were quite surprising! I discovered that although I love pattern; I actually prefer to wear items that are quite plain. I might go as far as a stripe or spots but geometrics or florals just didn't feature at all on my board – but they were in my wardrobe and these were the items that I just was not comfortable wearing.

The second thing that I noticed was that many of the items I had pinned were in neutrals – navy and charcoal in particular. Very few colours appeared on my board. It wasn't that I didn't like colour; I love colour but I prefer it in "pops" of colour rather than in blocks.

Getting clear on this enabled me to filter the items in my wardrobe and put together outfits that I loved. Most importantly, it stopped me from buying items that fell outside what has become my signature style. I will still pick up and admire a gorgeous floral dress or top, but knowing that I won't wear it – or if I do, feel uncomfortable in it, I leave it hanging in the store and go and find something that suits my style instead.

Colour Matters!

Often, when we feel self-conscious or we don't want to stand out, we opt for dark colours such as black so we blend in. But these colours can be harsh on many of us leaving us looking tired and drained, when instead wearing colours that complement us can help us to look younger, healthier and more refreshed – who would not want that!

Colour can make us look fabulous and feel better about ourselves too. I find that when I do wear colour, that it makes people smile. So often I hear people say that when they are feeling good, that they will go and wear something brighter and more cheerful – well why not try the same when you are having a not so good day and see if it positively impacts your mood?

When I work with my clients on their colour palettes, it never ceases to amaze me their reaction when they see the difference of wearing a colour that complements them against one that doesn't. When a colour works for them, it's like a lightbulb has gone off near their face, their skin can look clearer and their eye colour becomes more enhanced. For some of my clients, their posture completely changes too. One of my clients called her palette her "sit-up" colours because she recognised how different her posture was when she wore them. Knowing that a colour you are wearing suits you can help you to feel so much more confident.

We make all kinds of judgements about what colours we can wear – and those that we can't. Well, here is the shocker – you can wear any colour that you like! And yes, that goes for black too. It is the shade and the tone that is important, and also how you wear it.

What you want is for the colour you are wearing to work in harmony with your physical colouring. When you wear a colour neither you nor the colour should dominate, everything should be balanced. As a tip, you can do the "blink test". Put a colour near your face in front of a mirror then turn away and look back. If you see the colour first, the chances are that colour is too strong. However, if when you look back, you are looking at you as the whole, then this indicates the colour works for you.

It is also really easy to bring your colours into your existing wardrobe without spending a fortune. Jewellery and scarves are brilliant ways to add colour quickly and easily and are a great way to add impact to your outfit. I spend time with my clients helping them to understand how to combine colours so they can see how to accessorise and how to mix and match items into outfits so not only are they bringing in their colours but they are also getting more use out of the items that they already own. Then, when items need replacing, that's when they can add new items in their colours. This also allows my clients to experiment with their new colours in a way that feels safe. If they feel uncomfortable in a bright orange scarf at work, they can always take it off – not possible if they have opted for a bright orange dress.

Often when clients wear colours from their new palette, they are told that they "look well" and people will compliment them however, they do not necessarily know why that person looks so well that day as opposed to any other day. It's like your own secret weapon that you can chose to share with whom you please.

The other benefit of knowing the colours that look great on you is that when it comes to shopping, you can just walk straight on past those items that don't flatter you. You filter as you shop so the items that you take into the changing room are more likely to work for you – without all the drama. Great for the sales too! So many people avoid colour so when it comes to the sales, you can get some real bargains – especially online when items have been moved out of the store to make way for new lines, you will often still find sale items online so it is always worth having a browse and seeing what you can find.

Styles that Suit

Having got to grips with the types of clothes you like to wear and the colours that really work for you, the next step is to discover the styles of clothing that suit your body.

Normally this is done through body shapes – apple, pear, hourglass, athletic – there are various ways of describing body shapes but this is only part of the story. Explaining to one of my clients how to dress for her oval body shape, does not help her when she feels self-conscious about her arms, or her knees – you would be surprised the areas of the body that people feel self-conscious of!

I genuinely believe that in order to really dress with confidence, you need to know how to dress each part of your body separately so I prefer a head to toe approach which allows me to show my clients how to minimise a full bust, add curves to slim hips or distract attention from a part of their body that they feel self-conscious of. Stylists are simply masters of disguise! I can show you how to conceal those areas that you make you feel less confident whilst revealing those areas you are happy to show.

So, for example, I have curvy hips but sadly, was certainly nowhere to be found in the bust queue! However, whilst I feel self-conscious of my hips and thighs, I am happy to highlight my slimmer top half and I do have a nice defined waist so am happy to show that too. Therefore, I want to disguise my hips and highlight the top half of my body. I do this by wearing darker colours and keeping detail to minimum around my hips but wearing brighter, lighter colours and pattern on my top half to draw the eye upwards.

To show off my waist, I choose fabrics and styles that highlight it rather than styles that fall straight down and my waist is lost, making me lose my shape and actually making me look larger than I am.

Once I understand how my client feels about her body, I can then guide her on the styles of clothes that will work for her. However, whilst the style and shape of the garment is important, fabric is also really important! You can use fabric to really show off your figure to its best advantage.

Curvy figures look amazing in soft fabrics that drape such as jersey or a soft knit. These fabrics will skim the curves and really flatter. Whilst those with straighter figures who have very little definition at the waist and are neat on the hips and thighs, require stiffer fabrics such as linens and stiff cottons to give definition to their body shape. To create the illusion of a waist, a jacket in a stiff fabric with a nipped in waist will really flatter a straighter body shape.

Understanding how to dress your body to its best advantage is a great plus, but it also helps when you go shopping. You will be able to pick up an item in store and know if it will suit you or not before you get into the changing room making shopping so much easier too!

Turning Clothes into Outfits.
One of the favourite parts of what I do is editing peoples' wardrobes. It is such a privilege to do this as you get to discover so much about them and also peek into special times in their lives as you see the outfits they wore on their honeymoon, or a family wedding or a special date. No matter how many wardrobes they have (and some people have quite a few!) they are always such much fun to do.

What I do often find however, is that quite often people buy items as individual pieces and do not necessarily think about what they have that will go with it. Either that, or they buy a top to go with a pair of trousers and only wear it with those trousers; they struggle to see how they can integrate it more fully into their wardrobe.

I have recently done a challenge with some of my clients to help with this process. I asked them to take 10 items which could be made into 10 separate outfits over 10 days. With some thought about what activities they were doing over those 10 days and how they can mix and match colours and items, some did really well and completed the challenge whilst others felt that they were unable to start the challenge as they felt that did not have 10 items that they could move into different outfits – despite having many items of clothing. For this latter group, I believe that some my clients did have sufficient items but struggled to pull outfits together.

I often find that my clients want colours to match exactly. So they would look for a pair of trousers to go with a top that has a particular shade of blue in it. They may find the trousers but will then only wear those 2 items together and would not wear them with anything else they own. Colours do not have to match exactly. In fact, most people would not notice if they did or didn't match. Similar shades can work beautifully together.

Many people are not confident about combining colours so I go through this with my clients as this can open up a whole new dimension to your wardrobe. It also means that you get more outfits from what you already own and that you can have fewer items in your wardrobe.

I want my client's wardrobes to work as hard as my clients often do, and so I love to take their individual items and create stylish outfits with them. These outfits can then be photographed so my client can refer back to them when they need ideas.

Creating Capsules

This leads us onto capsule wardrobes. Capsule wardrobes are simply a compact collection of items that can easily be mixed and matched into several outfits meaning that you buy less and wear more, optimising the investment that you have made in your wardrobe. Especially great for ladies that work in a more formal environment where they may invest heavily in their work wardrobe.

Depending on your lifestyle, you may find that one capsule wardrobe will cover all areas of your life or if you spend your work and home lives very differently, then it may be difficult to do this and separate work and home capsules are required as there is little opportunity to share items across the different activities in your life – wearing your expensive suit to go paintballing with the kids or to your Pilates class is not a practical option!

Neutral colours should be the base of your capsule. Neutral colours are those such as navy, black or charcoal. The reason that they form the basis of your capsule is because neutral colours go with everything, including each other. Now, your colour palette will determine how best to combine colours for you but the basics remain the same.

Therefore, I recommend that any items that you can have in your wardrobe for a number of years or that you will be wearing a lot such as a winter coat or a suit for work, should be in a neutral colour that looks fabulous on you. If you chose, you can spend more on these items as the colour is a classic that is unlikely to look dated.

With neutral colours forming the basis of your wardrobe, you can then bring in other colours in your tops, dresses, scarves and jewellery knowing that they will easily go with your neutral basics.

If you are someone who likes to stay on trend and wear the latest colours and styles of the season, they you can opt to spend less on these items so if you chose, you can remove them from your wardrobe at the end of the season without too much heartache.

Here are some tips on creating a work capsule wardrobe:

- If you are working full time, I recommend 6 to 8 tops and dresses. This means that you have enough options for every day of the week without doing laundry. It also means that you have a couple of spares should you drop toothpaste down your front or accidentally draw on your top with a pen that is rolling off the table – yes, I have done both of those things just this week!
- For every bottom (skirt or trousers) you should have at least 3 tops that will go with it. This is building flexibility into your wardrobe and ensuring that each item that you own has earned its place in your collection.
- If you require a jacket for work, then I would recommend 2 or 3 in colours that easily go with your tops and dresses. This means that you can easily create an outfit – grab a pair of trousers, select a top and then a jacket and you are good to go. If a jacket is not required, you could swap this for cardigans instead.

This is great if you are travelling with work as you can easily mix and match items for a few days to get different outfits and different looks.

Capsule wardrobes are all about making getting dressed easy and maximising the investment you make in your clothes. They also help you to focus when you go shopping and can stop you making expensive mistakes buying items that you have nothing to go with and never wear.

The Power of Accessories

Jewellery, scarves, belts and bags are great ways to add interest to your outfit and take an everyday outfit and turn it into something so much more stylish.

The personal style exercise done earlier is really quite key here. Some people will love a statement piece of jewellery whilst someone else will prefer something much more understated. It is really important to get clear on this first before you start investing.

The other great thing about accessories is that we can use them to highlight particular areas of our body and distract from others. If you are full busted, a brooch worn higher up near the collar bone will take the eye away from the bust and towards your face – much more appropriate if in a work environment.

If you have a gorgeous defined waist, then the addition of a belt to a straight cut dress will highlight it beautifully. But if you feel self-conscious of your mid-section, then a beautiful statement necklace will take people's attention so they won't even glance anywhere else.

I love helping clients highlight their body shape with accessories. There's so much choice and I've seen such a difference when women start investing in accessories.

Accessories are a great way to add colour to an outfit too. Most people will have black in their wardrobe but for many of us, black on its own, next to our face, can be a little harsh. This does not mean that we should not wear it, it just means that when we do, we need to add some of our best colours to the outfit. A coloured scarf or necklace placed on a neutral outfit can really make a difference and it takes just seconds.

If you would love to wear a scarf but aren't sure how to wear it, there are plenty of videos online which will give you all the knowledge that you need; so get browsing.

If you are a woman that feels more comfortable wearing clothes in neutral shades, then you may prefer to add colour in bags or shoes or a scarf but tied to a bag rather than worn against you.

Whatever your style, age or shape, accessories can play a huge part in reinvigorating your wardrobe – and it doesn't have to be expensive. There are plenty of High Street stores offering some great options.

Often, accessories get worn for a while and then placed in a draw and forgotten about so it is worth having a look at what you already have; you might be surprised! If you have pieces that you know you will not wear again, now is the time to remove then and pass then onto someone that will love them. Then next time you go shopping, take some time to go and look in the accessory section too.

Make-up Can Be Your Friend

As someone who has struggled with acne from quite young, make-up has been a way of disguising my bad skin and it boosted my confidence dramatically. But even if you have perfect skin, a few touches of make-up in the right places to enhance your features can make quite an impact. The great thing about makeup is that you don't have to wear a lot if you don't want to but still achieve great results.

I often work with ladies who don't wear make-up but who would like to. With all the products available now, they just don't know where to start. Also ladies will confide in me that they are using the same make-up shades and applying in the same way that they did in their 20's. They are ready for a change and are wanting to update their look, discover what all these new products do and how to use them.

Sometimes it is just little tweaks such as showing a tired new Mum how to disguise dark circles under their eyes, or simply updating a lady's lipstick shade to one that is more flattering for her now that her hair has gone lighter. For others, it is an introduction to make-up for the very first time and it can be a fun and exciting journey of discovery for them. They may not wear it every day after the session, but if they choose too, they have the knowledge and skills to do so.

You see, this is where I think guys have it a little bit easier! As women that wear make-up, one of the first things that they do every day, is to look in a mirror and look for any marks, spots or dark circles just so that they can disguise them with make-up. We pro-actively look for any flaws which cannot be a great way to start the day. Guys, or most guys, will not have to go through this process. However, once those areas of concern are disguised, it can do wonders for our confidence and self-esteem.

Be Kind to Your Reflection

So whilst, we are talking about mirrors, let me digress just a little. So often clients will come to my studio and they will be chatty and fun – until I ask them to take their make-up off and sit in front of a mirror! At which point, some ladies will lean forward and point out the lines and marks and move the skin saying how they need a facelift whilst for others, their personality will completely change; for some, they will not even look in the mirror at all and will turn their bodies away as much as they can. When I am working with a client to create their colour palette, I need them to see how different colours work on them and for some, I can see that they really struggle with looking at their reflection.

But, I get it! When my skin was at its worst, I would train myself to wash my hands, do my hair and clean my teeth all without looking in the mirror! My Dad would not be able to comprehend how I could possibly leave the house with toothpaste round my mouth because he assumed I would look in a mirror either during cleaning my teeth or afterwards – but no, I had trained myself not to.

As women, we can be really hard on ourselves. When we look in the mirror, we look for any flaws, anything that has changed, the marks, the dark circles and we are super critical. But you know, when others look at us, they are looking at us as a whole. They are not looking for flaws, they are just looking at us.

If we were with a friend and she was looking in the mirror and pointing out areas that she didn't like, we would tell her not to be silly. We would say that she looks gorgeous and the things that she is pointing out we cannot see or just do not notice.

So if this sounds like you, I want you to start a new habit of being your own best friend when you look in the mirror. Do not concentrate on the things that you don't like, but point out things that you do! Your stunning eyes, great legs, toned arms. It will do wonders for your self-esteem and you will leave the house feeling much more positive. Try it!

The Unplanned Shopping Trip

When we go shopping without really planning, this is where expensive mistakes can be made. We come home empty handed, with a replica of things we already have or something "that will do".

These are all reasons why we end up with clothes that we don't wear, feel feed up with our wardrobe or have a wardrobe with barely anything in it! I meet so many ladies who just hate shopping for these reasons but a little research and preparation can make your trip so much shorter and even enjoyable.

When I do a personal shopping trip with a client, I will do plenty of research including, discovering what she already has in wardrobe, where there are any gaps and the types of clothes that she likes to wear. I will also do some online research before I go so I know which brands and stores are the best to visit.

So, here are some tips:

- You are going to be in front of a mirror when you are trying on, so take the time to do hair and make-up before you go.
- Go when you have time to browse – not when you have 20 minutes before picking up the kids or before the parking meter runs out. This is when you will make mistakes. If you can, go early in the week when it is quieter and take the time to browse.
- Please ask the Assistants for help if you need things in a different size. That is what they are there for.
- Go with a list of what you need and don't get distracted. If you have 5 pairs of navy trousers in the wardrobe, you do not need another pair – even if they

are half price and fit like a dream! When we find shopping for a particular item difficult (trousers for me), we can opt for the easy option and buy yet another top. But when we get home, we still don't have the item that we need and that makes our wardrobes more flexible. Stick with it and be prepared to try on different sizes and brands.

- Do some online research before you do. This will stop you from walking round stores that do not have what you want or styles that suit you. It is more productive if you head straight for the stores that are more likely to have what you need.

- Do try on instore. So many times I find items in wardrobes that do not get worn because they weren't right but never got taken back because of time, location or just because it didn't happen. There are so many better ways to spend your money than on clothes that never get worn.

The "Copy Cat" Experience

When we feel lost about what suits us or are ready for a change but don't know how, we can take inspiration from those around us; friends, family or celebrities. Whilst this is a good thing to do to discover the types of clothes we like, copying and expecting it to look fabulous, can be a huge mistake, just because we are all different. Our body shapes, our proportions, our style can be completely different so just because it looks great on someone else sadly, does not mean it will look great on you.

It is vital that you really understand what works for you, and you alone. Only then, will you really be able to dress in a way that makes you look and feel amazing! You are unique! Don't try to be anyone else other than you.

Hiding in Baggy Clothes

When we feel self-conscious about our bodies, maybe we have put on a little weight, the simplest thing to do, can be to wear loose clothing that hides that extra weight. The bad news is that actually hiding our shape in baggy outfits can in fact make us look bigger than we actually are – and no-one wants that!

I had a client who had been teased at school because, at the time, her bust was quite full. As an adult, feeling that her bust was still disproportionate to rest of her body, her way to disguise it, was to wear loose tops and dresses. However, this lady had the most incredible hour glass figure with a beautifully defined waist that was being completely hidden.

When I held the extra fabric at the back of her top so that her waistline was visible it was like she had been on an instant diet. And guess what, her bust was beautifully in proportion with her figure! To help her confidence, I was able to give her some tips on how to wear her clothes so that her bust was not highlighted so she could transition into wearing clothes which showed off her shape with confidence.

Even if your waist is not as defined as my client above, wearing clothing that hides your shape is not necessarily the right thing to do.

I get that it can be a huge leap of faith going from baggy clothes to something more fitting but I can show you how to do it in a way that feels comfortable for you. Once you start getting the compliments, it will be so worth it!

When to Splurge and When to Save

A £200 coat that gets worn 5 days a week, 15 weeks of the year for 5 years, is way cheaper than a £30 coat that gets worn just a few times and then discarded for something else. Try to think about cost per wear.

How many times are you realistically going to wear an item? If it something that is likely to get worn every week and could be a classic piece that could stay in your wardrobe for years without looking outdated, then if you can afford to, it may be worth investing in an item and spending more on it.

Something that you will wear for a season and then probably not again, then spend less and so when you send it off to the Charity Store, you can do so guilt free.

It's Not a Bargain if You Never Wear It!

Sale time can tempt us to purchase those items that we never really would have at full price. Great, if it is an investment piece that will form a key part of your wardrobe but if not, you really need to consider if you will wear it at all.

Quite often, sale pieces are the items I find buried in clients wardrobes with the tags still on! Instead of rushing to the tills with it, why not ask the Store to hold it for you for a couple of hours – most stores will be happy to do this for you. If you cannot get the item out of your head and it goes with other items you already own, you can easily go back and get it. If not, then leave it with the Store and go and find something you will love to wear instead.

If It Does Not Fit – Do Not Buy It
The other items that end up not being worn are the items we buy to "slim into". So here is what so often happens; the weight loss doesn't happen – life just gets in the way – or, it does happen but our shape changes and the item we bought just doesn't fit properly or suit our new shape.

Buy things that flatter the person you are now! When you feel happy and confident in yourself; that is often when the weight loss happens.

Then you can congratulate yourself with some pieces in your styles and shapes that flatter the new you.

The other thing that happens is that we buy something that needs altering –and then never get it altered. So once again, it stays unworn.

Alteration shops are popping up in towns and shopping centres so check out where one is near to you now so if you need one, you know exactly where to go.

Be honest with yourself. If you know that in reality, taking your item to get altered is just never going to happen, then please leave it store.

Myth Busting!

There is no such thing as a standard size!

So many ladies get hung up on the size label! If this is you, I really want you to know that there is no such thing as a standard size – not even within the same brand! On a shopping trip with a client, she was a large in one jumper and a small in another – both in the same brand! Go for fit over everything else and if the label really offends you, then just cut it out!

You do not need to spend a fortune

It is not about having a huge wardrobe or lots of money. It is about spending wisely and knowing what suits you. It is possible to have a smaller wardrobe but get more outfits than if you had with a full wardrobe. And it may be possible to do this from the items that you already have. I have done wardrobe edits with clients before and created plenty of stylish outfits from what they already own and they don't need to go shopping at all.

It is not about size!

I recently found a survey that showed that nearly half of the ladies surveyed felt that shopping would be easier if they had a different body. I found this really upsetting because size is nothing to do with looking amazing! No matter your age, shape or size, I promise you, that you can look fabulous. It is just about discovering what really flatters you. You need to shop your shape, not your size, discover your style – not copy anyone else's, and learn how to hide and highlight and then you can really dress with confidence.

But don't wait to lose weight before you invest in you and your wardrobe. Don't put off feeling more confident about how you look.

Personal Stylists are Not Just for Celebrities
Stylists like me are trained to show you how to make the very best of who you are today. This is not – and should not be just for the rich and famous. Everyone needs to know how to dress in a way that makes them look and feel fantastic!

I just love to share what I know because when a client dresses with confidence, for me, it is the best feeling in the world.

I get some amazing feedback from some of my clients about how discovering what really suits them can help them going forward from starting new careers, rebuilding their confidence after being bullied at work, feeling more confident and increasing their self-esteem.

Getting dressed is so much more than just clothes.

Client Stories

One of my clients, Vanessa called me on the day of a friends Hen Do. She had a couple of hours to go before she needed to leave but she had no idea what to wear. She explained that she had just a few items in her wardrobe but she did not know if they suited her and they were not suitable for a special occasion anyway. She was waiting for her Mum to arrive with some of her clothes which she would borrow so that she could go to the event.

Vanessa was desperate to make a change and would go shopping but even if she picked items up, scared of making yet another mistake, she put them back and left the store empty-handed.

To increase the pressure on Vanessa, her workplace had decided to do away with uniforms meaning that she would now how to decide what to wear every day which simply felt overwhelming. Her uniform was her security, if it was wrong, it was not her fault! However, in just a few weeks, she would not be able to hide behind that any longer and her anxiety about what to wear was increasing.

Vanessa's biggest stumbling block, was that she had no idea what her style was. Therefore, when she went shopping, she felt completely overwhelmed by all the choices with no idea about how she wanted to look or what flattered her.

Our first session was helping Vanessa to get clear on her style. I promised her that she did have one – and she did! We discovered that Vanessa loves outfits in neutral shades with just pops of colour that add intrigue to her outfit. She did not particularly like patterns or frills, just plain items that looked really chic when out together.

Understanding her colour palette helped Vanessa to realise why some of the items she had in her wardrobe made her look washed out. Once she knew her colour palette, Vanessa was able to pick out some key neutral shades which would form the basis of her wardrobe and bring in pops of colour and pattern in accessories and footwear.

As someone that regularly worked out, Vanessa had a gorgeous figure - a beautiful hourglass. I showed her that by choosing fabrics that accommodated her curves, she would show off her fabulous figure and look slimmer because people could actually see her shape. Vanessa brought with her a jumper that had been gifted to her but she said each time she put it on, she took it off again as it didn't look right and she did not understand why. When she tried it on, the jumper was beautiful but was really chunky and with no real shape. It completely hid Vanessa's shape and the colour was not great for her either.

When it came to make-up, Vanessa had a very light complexion in contrast to her very dark hair and bright blue eyes. The foundations that she was using were too dark for her pale skin and by using shades that complimented her skin tone and features, her eye colour was enhanced and she just looked so much healthier and refreshed.

Vanessa had a wedding coming up in which her partner was best man so she was keen to ensure that she was dressed appropriately. She already had a gorgeous navy dress which we "wintered up" with navy opaques and ankle boots. Vanessa then purchased a beautiful bright pink coat to wear in the church as it was a winter wedding.

Vanessa said that although she felt a little self-conscious initially in such bright colours she got loads of compliments – including from her partners father who said she looked like a celebrity and who very nearly walked straight past her!

Vanessa is now gradually building up her wardrobe with pieces that she loves to wear. She knows her signature style and she knows the colours and styles of clothes that suit her. Shopping is no longer fruitless and she wears her own clothes when she goes out!

Another of my clients, Andi, is a Trainer, Speaker and Author in the Finance Industry. Andi was growing her business and was being asked to do much more public speaking and face-to-face marketing.

Andi contacted me because she had an Industry event to go to. She had been the previous year but when she arrived in her black suit and white top, she was horrified to notice that most of the other ladies were dressed very differently with dresses, lots of colour and accessories. Andi felt really self-conscious and it really impacted her confidence over the whole of the event. Andi was there to tell Companies what she did and market her service so needed to be at the top her game.

Not wanting to feel the same this year, Andi decided to make a change and signed up with me on a yearlong programme.
As the business trip was pending, we had to move our focus to this event so we started with a wardrobe edit. Andi had 2 wardrobes – which were very different! Her work wardrobe consisted of black suits and an array of white tops – lots of white tops.

On the weekends, Andi spent much of her time cycling but when I looked in her casual wardrobe which was formed mostly of sportswear, it was full of colour! It was like the wardrobes belonged to 2 completely different people!

In order to get clear on Andi's style, she had collected images from magazines of outfits that she liked and I was a little surprised to see that the images she had selected were still black and white. As she was in the Finance Industry, Andi felt that she should look like everyone else and that's what they wore.

I asked Andi to give me some words of how she would like to people describe her in business. She used words like inspirational, fun and positive but these words were not reflected at all in her business clothing.

Andi's colouring is really quite light so the black and white was really quite harsh on her. I showed her how lighter colours really lit up her face and also explained that black and white was quite an authoritative combination (think Police uniforms!) and that as a Trainer, some softer colours and more tonal colour combinations would make her look not only more approachable but also be much more fitting with the words she used to used previously.

Andi had also shied away from make-up in the past so I showed her a really simple make-up that complimented her colouring and that made her look a bit more polished so perfect for work.

Andi had quite an overwhelming day but she was also excited to get going to find her outfits for her business trip.

So, next we did a shopping trip. In her wardrobe there was one grey suit which she had been persuaded to purchase by her Mum and we decided to use this as a basis for her capsule wardrobe to take away with her.

As charcoal is a neutral colour it goes with everything so I picked out a number of tops in Andi's colours that would work with her suit. There were blues, pinks, corals and even some florals. Andi was amazed at the difference that the colours made and it did not take long to find a selection of tops that not only looked amazing, but could be packed without creasing so low maintenance too.

Andi was set for her business trip. She contacted me whilst she was there to say what a different that it made. Not only did she feel that she fitted in, but that she felt really confident when meeting people she had not met before and when presenting herself to prospective clients.

"What a life-transforming adventure it has been working with Rosie …. It has been a tremendously fun experience so far! And it has been transformational in terms of my confidence when I attend business development meetings, summits and networking events, etc."
Andi Lonnen – www.financetrainingacademy.com

Now the trip is over, Andi is working through the rest of her programme with me so by the end of the year, she will have a wardrobe of clothes she loves in colours that make her glow and in styles that flatter her shape. Andi made such a huge shift in such a short time but that leap of faith paid dividends in how confident she felt when it really mattered.

Can I be of help to you?

If any of this sounds like you, I would love to see if I can help.

Check out my website **www.rosiehuckle.com** where you can find out more about me, more about the services that I offer and find out how I have been able to help other women by reading their stories.

In brief, the services that I offer are:

Styling for Events:

Have you got an invite to a special event such as wedding, an event for work or even a TV appearance? Excited about going but deciding what to wear is really getting you down? I have created a package of services that will ensure that you look both appropriate and fabulous so you can relax and just enjoy your special day.

Styling for Confidence:

Create your signature style, discover your colour palette and learn how to dress your body to its very best advantage so you can really dress with confidence. I am with you every step of the way to support you as you transition into the new you.

Styling for Success:

Are you in the corporate world and great at what you do but worried that your appearance may be letting you down? Or do you have your own business and want to ensure that your appearance reflects your brand values? My Styling for Success programme may just be what you need.

If you are ready to get in touch, then you can email me on **hello@rosiehuckle.com** or call me on **07980 621989** and lets set up a no-obligation call to find out more about you and if I can help.

38581508R00022

Printed in Poland
by Amazon Fulfillment
Poland Sp. z o.o., Wrocław